SAVE A DRIVER'S LIFE

Important Strategies to Teach a New Driver Now!

By Hank Wysocki

Copyright © 2016

by Hank Wysocki

To Learn More

WWW.DRIVEREDCOACH.COM

Disclaimer

All rights reserved. This book or any portion of this book may not be reproduced in any form or manner without the expressed written permission of the publisher and author. No part of this publication may be reproduced in any form or by any means which includes electronic, photocopying, recording or transmitted by email without expressed written permission from the publisher.

While all attempts have been made to verify the information provided in this publication, the author assumes no responsibility for errors, omissions, or differing opinions and interpretations of the subject matter.

This book is solely for the purpose of information, education, and entertainment. The views expressed are those of the author. Reader ultimately is responsible for their own actions. The author and publisher specifically disclaim any responsibility for any liability, loss or risk, personal or otherwise which is incurred as a consequence, directly or indirectly of the use or application of any of the contents of this book.

Adherence to all applicable laws and regulations, including international, federal, state, and local governing professional licensing, business practices, advertising, and all other aspects of doing business in the US, Canada, or any other jurisdiction is the sole responsibility of the reader or purchaser. Neither the author nor the publisher assumes any responsibility or liability whatsoever on the behalf of the purchaser or reader of these materials. Any perceived slight of any individual or organization is purely unintentional.

INTRODUCTION

Over 60,000 drivers are killed each year in auto accidents. Thousands more are injured, costing our nation billions of dollars. Young drivers make up one of the largest group of contributors to these statistics. Auto crashes remain the leading cause of death of teenagers. Poor judgments, inexperience, as well as the low rate of seat belt usage are major factors contributing to these statistics. Insurance agencies have proclaimed the 16-25 age group "the risk pool" and as a result young drivers pay much higher insurance premiums for the *privilege* of driving on our nation's highways.

Our governing agencies have reacted to this problem by raising the driving age requirements and adding more stringent tests, but these two actions alone have not done enough to stop this major societal problem. Education and experience are the best approach to this crisis. Unfortunately, classrooms in driver education are deemed unnecessary in school budgets, and are often the first programs to be cut in secondary schools. Private driving schools often now assume the responsibility for the education of our young drivers. However, too many driving schools place a primary emphasis on passing the road test at the expense of teaching all of the necessary driving skills and techniques. The high cost of private driving lessons is also out of reach for many families in our country.

So, in a world with very few formal driver education programs in schools, where do we turn? Since driver education is unlikely to be returning to our school districts, the burden of educating young drivers will lie with parents, guardians, and relatives of these new drivers. While many adults see themselves as safe drivers, the reality is that they have not been trained effectively in the techniques of educating our young driving population. It is true that many adults mean well, and want their children to be safe behind the wheel, but unfortunately they lack the knowledge necessary to teach new drivers. If you find yourself in this category, do not worry, this book will help you. The combination of experience you have acquired over the many years of driving, along with the lessons and strategies offered in this book, will help you become a confident and comfortable instructor for your young driver. I hope you enjoy this book as much as I have enjoyed writing "Save Your Teenage Driver's Life" for you.

WHY I WROTE THIS BOOK

As an experienced driver education instructor for over 30 years I have witnessed the demise of our "in school" driver education programs. These programs provided teenage drivers with the necessary skills to navigate our nation's highways. The primary burden has now been placed on the parents of these new drivers. In order to properly educate your child, it is important for parents to make sure they are teaching all the necessary modern day driving techniques correctly. It is also important for all adults to be role models for their teenage drivers every time they get into a car. This book is intended to help guide and teach the important lessons necessary in order to help our young drivers to survive on our often dangerous roads and highways. These strategies, techniques, and practices must be taught and reinforced every time you go driving with your teenager. Understand that learning to drive is an ongoing process and the more a young driver practices, the more experience that is gained. "Save Your Teenage Driver's Life" will focus on the nine most critical elements of good driving behavior that every new driver needs to be taught. There is no "fluff" just the important information you need to teach your teenage driver now.

WHY YOU SHOULD READ THIS BOOK

If you could help prevent your son or daughter from being involved in a fatal or injury producing collision, would you? Hopefully your answer to this question is a resounding, "Yes of course." Did you know that eighty percent of all accidents (collisions) on our nation's highways are preventable if only you apply a few simple driving strategies? Driver education classes, and private driving lessons alone, will not be enough to help our children navigate today's complex highway transportation system. It is the parent's job to reinforce, and to model the vital skills necessary to help develop educated confident young drivers. Learning and reinforcing the skills taught by a professional instructor has now become an important role of the parent. There is no substitute for experience. Twenty minutes of driving in a driver education car or a one hour driving lesson with a professional teacher is not nearly enough time. The parent must supplement these lessons with continuous road practice. If you are not fortunate enough to have a driver education program in your area then it will become your job to learn all the important strategies involved with defensive driving. "Save Your Teenage Driver's Life" will teach you these strategies, as well as serve as an important reminder of which driving techniques you should be modeling properly for your child. Each chapter will provide a valuable lesson for both you and your new driver. It is important that both the adult and teenager read this book and apply all the important lessons that are offered. Read and learn these lessons carefully and continue to reinforce them on a daily basis until they become habit. In the last section of the book I have provided you with a valuable checklist to serve as a reminder of all these key lessons. You can also download and copy this list, along with a copy of my "Keys to Passing the Road Test Guide," at www.driveredcoach.com

How This Book Is Organized

"Save Your Teenage Driver's Life" is set up in short easy to read chapters. Each chapter is designed to reinforce the important components of proper driver education strategies and techniques. Chapter One covers the basic physical skills that all new drivers need to learn before they hit the roads. Chapters Two and Three deal with the two key defensive concepts of *following distance* and *visual lead time*. In Chapter Four you will learn what safety features are available in all new cars and how to properly use them in the event a collision should ever occur. Chapters Five and Six deal with two of the most trending problems all new drivers are faced with today, alcohol and driver distraction. Chapter Seven tackles the topic of how to deal with some common driving emergencies. Chapter Eight discusses aggressive driving, as well as the important subject of attitude behind the wheel. Finally, in Chapter Nine we tie it all together in a handy checklist to reinforce all of these essential "lifesaving topics." "Save Your Teenage Driver's Life" will touch on all the important lessons new drivers need to be taught now. The earlier your young driver is taught these important lessons, the more prepared, and better skilled, they will be. Parents and new drivers can work together to establish proper driving habits and techniques, to make sure everyone is safer on our nation's highways.

About the Author

Hank Wysocki has been involved with Driver and Traffic Safety Education for over thirty years. He is a New York State certified Driver Education instructor as well as an Instructor for the New York State Pre-licensing program. Hank is also certified by Driver Training Associates as a qualified instructor of the Point and Insurance Reduction Program. Hank has taught thousands of students in both the classroom and behind the wheel. He is also an active proponent of parent involvement within the entire driver education process for all beginning drivers. "Saving Your Teenage Driver's Life" is the first book in a series of educational resources designed by Hank Wysocki to help promote, and educate everyone on the strategies and techniques of proper driving technique. The author hopes readers will incorporate these techniques and strategies to form a critical partnership with teenage drivers. If there is private driving instructor or public school driving teacher involved with your teenager's education be sure to reinforce the lessons that they teach along with the strategies within this book. Also, be sure to provide your new driver with plenty of practice time in order to reinforce proper defensive driving habits. Good habits are formed early, and driver education is an ongoing process. Practice does not make perfect. Correct practice makes for a perfect and necessary life skill.

TABLE OF CONTENTS

INTRODUCTION	4
ABOUT THE AUTHOR	11
TABLE OF CONTENTS	13
CHAPTER 1: THE BASICS	14
CHAPTER 2: FOLLOWING DISTANCE	20
CHAPTER 3: VISUAL LEAD TIME	26
CHAPTER 4: SAFETY RESTRAINT SYSTEMS	31
CHAPTER 5: ALCOHOL AND THE NEW DRIVER	36
CHAPTER 6: DISTRACTED DRIVING	41
CHAPTER 7: EMERGENCY PROCEDURES	45
CHAPTER 8: ATTITUDE AND DRIVING	53
CHAPTER 9: A LIFESAVING CHECKLIST	56
DRIVER EDUCATION RESOURCES	59

1: THE BASICS

...any years, and enormous amounts of money educating our students on subjects such as reading, writing, science and math. Yet a high percentage of our nation's youth never receive any formal driver education training. This is unfortunate since driving a 2000 pound vehicle is a monumental task and if performed improperly can result in injury or death! Learning the proper skills and techniques of driving will help to reduce the number of traffic fatalities on our roads and highways. Let's take a look at some of the skills that should be taught to every beginning driver. Remember that there are three controls that every driver always has; braking, steering and acceleration. Learning the proper use of these controls can go a long way in the prevention of an accident.

Hand Placement on Steering Wheel

Driving experts seem to agree that the hands must be placed high on the steering wheel for maximum control! Teach your new driver to place both their hands high on the steering wheel. The left hand placed at 9:00, and the right hand placed at 3:00, is the preferred position for a maximum turning radius. A 10:00 left hand position, with a 2:00 right hand position, is also acceptable if that is more comfortable. By placing hands high on the wheel you will not only achieve maximum turning radius, but you will also save valuable time in the case of any evasive maneuver. The hands must always return to the upper half of the wheel in order to maintain optimal steering control, and to help avoid critical objects in the vehicles path. Picture a young driver with their hands low on the wheel. A deer runs out into their path, and now they must return their hands to the top of the wheel in order to avoid the crash. While their hands are moving to the upper half of the wheel the car continues to move. This movement takes time. And time means distance. This critical time could have been used to help prevent the collision. Think about it, have you ever seen a race car driver with their hands on the bottom of the wheel? Start the hands where they will finish, on the upper half of the wheel.

Braking

The average driver reaction is about ¾ of a second. Now remember that is the average of all drivers. Some people may be faster while others are considerably slower. Reaction time is the time when you first discover an obstacle in your driving path, and you immediately move your foot over the brake pedal without physically pressing it. This movement takes an average of ¾ of a second for most drivers. Which in reality means that your car continues to move as your foot goes from the gas pedal to the brake. Most drivers fail to calculate this important distance. Just like steering, the critical reaction time distance can be the difference between life and death. The AAA Traffic Safety Department has developed a chart that provides minimum stopping distances for passenger cars. This chart shows that a normal car with good brakes takes up to 260 feet to come to a stop at 60 miles per hour. Within this total stopping distance are two very important components. The first one is reaction time distance. Again, this is the distance that involves moving your foot from the gas pedal to the brake without physically pressing the brake. Believe it or not that distance is 66 feet at a speed of sixty miles an hour! Your car then travels another 194 feet after you have depressed the brakes. This distance may also include a skid. That makes for a total stopping distance of 260 feet! This important fact makes it crucial to teach new drivers that the brakes stop the wheels, not the car!

Ok, so what is proper braking technique? You really only have two choices, your right foot or your left foot. Most experts agree that the right foot doing everything (acceleration and braking) is the way to go. Numerous studies have shown even with the left foot resting on the brake, the right foot is considerably faster. Besides, "left foot brakers", "ride the brake" illuminating their brake lights, and wearing out their brake pads much faster. Teach your new driver to brake with the right foot only.

THE EYES

Scanning the traffic scene with your eyes is arguably one of the most important skills a new driver should develop. The eyes are continuously moving, looking for any problems that may be encountered in front of the car as well as behind the car. They should never fixate on any one object. Checking the speedometer, or changing a radio station, should be done quickly so that the eyes can get back onto the roadway where they belong. When driving in reverse it is important to turn around and look in the direction that you are moving. You should never just rely on the mirrors when driving in reverse.

SPEED CONTROL

Maintaining a proper speed for the road quality and weather conditions is a skill that all new drivers must continuously develop. Our local towns and cities provide all the signs necessary to keep traffic flowing smoothly at safe speeds. Common sense is necessary when conditions change based on the road surface, temperature, and weather. Slowing down gradually, and avoiding quick accelerations away from traffic lights and stop signs, are important safety habits which go a long way in saving fuel. Learn to drive as a "loner". In other words try to avoid driving in close proximity to other drivers. Be an anti-social driver! This means keeping as much space around your entire car as physically possible. Less can go wrong, and accidents become less severe, when you have more space to work with.

LATERAL MANEUVERS

When we talk about lateral maneuvers we are simply talking about any time you make a lane change or move the car from one side of the road to the other. The approved technique for a lateral maneuver is to signal first, check your rear view mirror second, and finally check your blind spot before actually moving. This technique must be followed in this exact order every time without exception. The blind spot is referred to as the two points off of the rear bumper that cannot be seen in the rear view mirror. The blind spot makes it possible for other vehicles to be driving alongside your car without you ever knowing it. That is why it is critical to make a quick check over our right or left shoulder as a final important action before completing your lateral maneuver.

Chapter 2: Following Distance

How far you follow behind other vehicles is the single most important accident prevention strategy that should be taught to all new drivers. Keeping a safety cushion in front of our car goes a long way in preventing collisions. It gives our eyes the precious time needed to react to any obstacles in your driving path. It also gives you the space needed to make a safe stop should the vehicle in front of you brake abruptly. Besides, ninety nine percent of all collisions in which the driver from behind hits the driver in front is the fault of that tailgating driver. Not only are they at fault, but they will most likely be ticketed for their actions. Using a proper following distance also gives you time to brake effectively if a problem develops farther up the road. Dropping back allows us better overall visibility, around, and in front of the car ahead of us. Trucks or large vehicles will require a greater following distance based on their size. Dropping back allows you to see around that large vehicle, as well increasing the chance that the truck driver will be able to see you. Side view mirrors only allow limited view to the rear for most large vehicles. Following distance allows you to see and be seen. You never want to hide in traffic.

You want to make your presence known on the roads at all times. Daytime driving lights and proper road positioning allow you to be seen more easily, and in turn makes for a safer driving experience.

So how far is the accepted following distance behind another motor vehicle? The answer to that question depends on many factors. Two of these factors were mentioned above: 1. How big is the vehicle ahead of you? (The larger the vehicle the farther we drop back) and 2. What type of roads are you driving on? Dirt roads may require a greater following distance. Weather is also a huge factor in our following distance decision. Snow, ice and rain are all factors that require us to rethink our following distance choice.

All driving experts agree that this "space cushion" must increase as vehicle speeds increase. In previous decades, driver education teachers instructed new drivers to use one car length of following distance for every ten miles an hour of speed. While this may be sound advice, most people have difficulty approximating what this distance really looks like. When a vehicle is moving, it is very difficult to determine car length distance. A great example of this difficulty is when I recently polled my driver education class on the length of the dotted white lines on our nation's expressways. I asked them how long that they thought each dotted line was. The average guess was anywhere from one foot to ten feet. The reality is that these lines are fifteen feet long, reaffirming the belief that distance calculations are very difficult to determine in a moving car.

Two Second Rule

The modern accepted way to determine the distance you need to be driving behind another vehicle is called the "two second rule." Two seconds is the required space needed when traveling on dry roads behind another car at speeds of forty five miles an hour or less. Ok, so how do we determine what a two second following distance looks like? It's actually pretty simple. When the car in front of you passes a fixed object on, or near the side of the road, you count one thousand one, one thousand two and then your car passes this same fixed object on or near the side of the road. You can use a tree, a pole, a sign or some sort of a road marking to serve as your fixed object. Remember to continue to maintain this space even if the vehicle in front of you slows down. This two second "space cushion" will give you plenty of time to stop if the car in front of you slams on their brakes for any reason.

Four Second Rule

Once we get out on the highways and freeways our speeds begin to increase. Two seconds will no longer serve the purpose. You should now increase your following distances to four seconds for speeds over forty five miles an hour on dry pavement. Braking and skidding distances also increase substantially at these higher speeds. Keeping this four second "space cushion" allows you time to check instruments and mirrors and also provides you adequate time to slow down in case the vehicle in front of you should slam on their brakes. When teaching young drivers about expressway following distances it is also important to reinforce the skill of driving as a "loner." Driving as a loner means avoiding other cars, and becoming "anti- social" on our modern high speed roadways. Isolate your vehicle by avoiding the packs of cars bunched together with little or no following distance. If necessary, you can also drop back behind these packs of drivers or accelerate around them. Always remember to maintain this cushion even if the driver in front of you slows down. Your following distance stays with you no matter what speeds you are traveling at.

Bad Weather

Bad weather presents many problems for not only new drivers, but even for the most experienced of drivers. Your visibility decreases in rain and snow, and the pavement becomes slicker. The best strategy is to avoid driving in these conditions. Unfortunately we cannot always do that. If we must tackle hazardous road conditions, a six second following distance is acceptable for rain and snow. At least eight seconds is needed for icy conditions. This is also a good time to teach young drivers about the proper use of an ice scraper, the defroster systems, and the value of good wiper blades. Having the appropriate set of tires, as well as acceptable tread depth, are very important for traction in adverse driving conditions. Never set off on a journey in bad weather without clearing every aspect of the front, rear, and side windows. Visibility is extremely important. So make sure your headlights are on, so that your vehicle can easily be seen.

Night Time and Fog

Fog and night time driving are two very unique situations. First and foremost your headlights must always be on in these conditions. Your low beam headlights can only project out a specified distance making your overall visibility a lot trickier. You do not want to "overdrive" your headlights. Overdriving your headlights simply means driving faster than the actual projection rate of the headlights themselves. In other words you reach objects in your path before you physically see them. It is recommended that you use a four second following distance during night time driving. Immediately reestablish this four second following distance in your own car to check if this is adequate for your own personal night driving needs. High beams should be used as much as possible. Make sure to click down to your low beams when you meet an oncoming car. That way you won't blind the other driver and make their problem your problem.

When driving in fog always use your low beam headlights. High beams are ineffective since the particles of light are reflected back toward your car making it more difficult to see. Night driving requires a minimum four second following distance. Driving in fog should mandate at least a space cushion of six seconds or more. Again, remember to "see and be seen."

Chapter 3: Visual Lead Time

In addition to *following distance*, probably the next most important skill that all young drivers should learn is the establishment of a proper *visual lead time*. Or, in other words, how far down the road you should be searching. A *visual lead time* provides two important functions. The first is that it allows you to keep your vehicle in a straight line path. Most beginning drivers typically use search patterns that reach only a few yards past the hood of their cars. This restricted view causes them to hug one side of the road or possibly causes them to weave from one side of the road to the other. Looking farther down the road aligns the car in a straight line path.

The second and perhaps more important reason is that proper visual lead time allows you to identify any problems occurring farther down the road. Early detection allows you time to decide on any further action that may need to be taken. The action could be braking or perhaps even changing a lane. *Visual lead time* not only allows you to see the road ahead, but also provides a driver with the added visibility to see both sides of the road.

With the eyes up and looking down the road, problems can be avoided well in advance. In city situations where there are double parked cars, traffic lights, signs, and road markings, the lead time offers important clues early in your visual patterns. Early recognition allows us to slow down or change lanes well in advance, so the driver can avoid last second risky maneuvers. In the suburbs, cross walks, pedestrians and animals all can become hazards if not identified early. On high speed highways, directional signs, the lanes alongside your car, as well as the vehicles in front and behind you, can all offer important early clues to any problems that could be encountered in your driving path.

Driving search patterns, when cultured early, can go a long way in the prevention of fatal collisions, and injury producing accidents. The eyes should be continuously moving and should never be fixated on any one object. Checking vehicle instruments and mirrors should all be done in a split second. New drivers must learn to take a defensive posture when on the roads at all times. In other words, they are looking for other drivers to make mistakes and not always assuming they will be making safe driving choices. A defensive driver identifies problems early, makes critical speed adjustments and executes lane changes when necessary.

Twelve Second Rule

How is a visual lead time determined? Since it is impossible to calculate distance when you are driving a vehicle at high speeds, you can again use the method of counting seconds in order to determine what your optimal visual lead time should be. Counting seconds only needs to be performed once in order to determine your own personal visual lead time.

Twelve seconds or more is the recommended visual lead time for speeds under 45 miles per hour. In order to calculate this lead time, just go out for a drive in a location where speed limits are below 45, such as a city or suburban area. With your eyes up, pick the farthest point out that you can see within your visual search pattern. Once you have picked out an object such as a sign, light post or parked car, begin counting one thousand one, one thousand two, until you reach one thousand twelve. You should reach the object you have selected either at or beyond your twelve second count. If your search pattern is well short of the twelve seconds, then try it again until you have a minimum of twelve seconds. Once you figure out what your lead time distance is, begin to work on this new habit right away, and make it consistent every time you drive. The only way to establish a new positive habit is by repetition. Continue to practice until your *visual lead time* is totally perfected. Being able to identify hazards and objects early in your visual path is a critical skill for all drivers.

TWENTY SECOND RULE

As you probably guessed, as your speed increases, so does the rate that you will reach critical objects and hazards within your driving path. For speeds over forty five miles an hour use the twenty seconds rule as your baseline visual target. These speeds are most frequently realized on high speed highways and multi-lane expressways. You will calculate your visual lead time exactly the same way you did with city and suburban speeds. The only notable difference is that your eyes are now scanning twenty or more seconds down the road. A roadway sign or mile marker makes a great reference point for calculating your twenty second visual lead time. Once you have checked "it", modify "it" and practice "it" so that "it" fits into the parameters of twenty seconds or more.

As we mentioned earlier, isolating your vehicle on high speed roadways is essential in safe driving practices. It is a lot less likely for an accident to occur, when fewer vehicles are surrounding you. Keeping space around, in front, and behind you, gives you many escape choices should a driving emergency occur. On multi-lane highways the middle lane is a great choice provided you are traveling at the speed of traffic. The middle lane gives you two escape routes right and left, as well as an optimal search visibility pattern.

Safe driving involves identifying objects early in our visual search patterns. If we do see something we don't like, it is pretty easy to adjust your speed or change your lane position to avoid the hazard. Predicting what other drivers will do is a strategy that needs to be developed and refined as new drivers gain experience. Remember eighty percent of all accidents are preventable simply by adjusting your vehicle well in advance of the sign of trouble.

Chapter 4: Safety Restraint Systems

Motor vehicle crashes are the leading cause of death for young drivers ages eighteen to twenty four. So it is also no surprise that these young drivers have the lowest compliance rate for safety belt usage. Immaturity and inexperience are two of the major contributors of collisions for new drivers. Seat belt laws have helped with compliance rates, but adults must continue to reinforce the importance of wearing a seat belt to our young driving population.

Using seat belts reduces the rate of fatality producing car crashes by over forty five percent according to the Center of Disease Control. Seat belts prevent bad accidents from becoming a lot worse. Convincing people to use them has been the primary battle. Seatbelts were first made mandatory in all new cars back in 1964. Unfortunately less than 10% of the national population used them at this time. According to the New York State Department of Motor Vehicles that number hovered between 10-16% up until 1984. Results were similar nationally. With the emergence of seat belt laws around the country these numbers have risen to between 85-91% today. The message needs to continue to spread until all vehicle occupants are restrained.

How Seat Belts Protect You

There are basically three parts to every motor vehicle crash. The first part is your car striking an object, such as a tree or another vehicle. The second part is your body striking the interior of your own car, and the third (proclaimed by doctors) is your internal organs colliding with your exterior parts (ribcage, bones, etc.). You need to prevent the second collision in order to survive the crash, and seat belts, along with air bags, give you the best chance. Everything unrestrained in a motor vehicle becomes a projectile in a collision. Unbuckled people become "human projectiles." To put this in perspective if a car travels at sixty miles an hour, and then the brakes are slammed on, everything in that vehicle travels at sixty miles an hour. That is just simple physics. So in reality you have to survive the collision from within your own car.

Safety belts will prevent the second collision. They will keep you in place and make sure you do not impact the windshield, dash, and steering wheel. By keeping you behind the wheel, seat belts give you the ability to maintain control of your car. Picture a race car driver when involved in a crash, spinning around or perhaps even flipping over. This driver even when dealing with a life threatening crash is still able to maintain control of their car. Perhaps most importantly, seat belts will prevent you from being ejected from the vehicle. You are more likely to be killed or injured seriously if you are thrown out of the vehicle. Seatbelts also help to put you in a more defensive posture by keeping you upright and alert.

There are two other actions all drivers should perform before leaving their driveway, the first is adjusting the headrest, and the second is locking your doors. Adjusting your headrest to the middle of your head helps prevent the neck from violently snapping back (whiplash). Locking your doors keeps you in the vehicle and helps prevent ejection. Any action regarding safety that must be taken before by the driver leaves the driveway or parking lot is called an active restraint. The action is active because you must physically perform these checks to ensure your safety. Modern car design has also included many features within the car to help passengers avoid serious injury in a collision. These designed features in your vehicle are called passive restraints because there is nothing the driver has to do physically. The car engineer has already done everything for the vehicle operator.

Passive Restraints

Since the late 1980's airbags have become the most popular form of passive restraints. These passive restraints have become standard in all new cars and have saved thousands of lives. Airbags have also have been shown to be extremely effective in the most dangerous crash of all; the head on collision. Designers continue to improve the safety of new vehicles by adding airbags to the driver and passenger side doors.

Recessed door locks and door handles have also become a very effective passive design in modern cars. In much older vehicles, drivers and passengers would be severely injured by door handles and locks that protruded out into the vehicle. Collapsible steering wheels are also a great design feature. These steering wheels are much softer and they "give" with the driver should they be involved in a motor vehicle crash. Padded dashboards also provide added protection in the event of the second collision.

New drivers should get into the habit early of taking care of all the active restraint protocol before they even head out onto the streets. Adults should set the example by performing these responsibilities each and every time. New drivers are constantly watching what the adults do. Adults are role models at all times whether they like it or not. Belts in combination with air bags give you the best chance for survival in a serious crash.

Chapter 5: Alcohol and The New Driver

Why is this chapter relevant if the legal drinking age in most states is twenty one? Time to wake up my friends; according to the 2014 National Survey on Drug Use and Health over 8.7 million people ages twelve to twenty have consumed alcohol. This is a huge problem. This becomes even more serious when these young people approach driving age. The driving age in most states is age sixteen. The National Highway and Traffic Safety Administration reports that the age sixteen through twenty-four age group is responsible for thirty-two percent of all fatal car crashes. We cannot hide from these sobering statistics and as parents and adults we need to approach these facts, and deal with them head on. Pretending there is not a problem never really solves the problem.

Underage drinking is only part of the challenge. The decision to get in a car and drive after drinking is a much bigger consequence. DWI (Driving While Intoxicated) or DUI (Driving Under the Influence), has been a major crisis in American society. Stricter laws and educational programs have been able to gradually reverse the crisis. Unfortunately, the number of drinking driving accidents in this country still hovers around forty five percent. There is still much work to be done in order to help solve this major societal problem. The average cost of a first time DWI is around ten thousand dollars when considering lawyer fees, insurance costs, lost wages and re-licensing fees.

So as parents and adults how do we approach this topic with your teenage drivers? I have had the good fortune, as a teacher and administrator to work with an organization called SADD. SADD stands for Students Against Destructive Decisions. This organization was originally set up in 1981 as an organization committed to spreading the awareness of the many problems associated with drinking, drugs and driving. SADD has since expanded its focus to include not only traffic safety, drug and alcohol abuse, but also has gotten involved with many other pertinent health issues which teenagers face on a daily basis. All across our nation SADD has empowered young people to take the lead in important education and prevention programs within their own schools and communities. This organization was instrumental in creating drinking and driving contracts between parents and their young drivers. A signed commitment was established prompting young drivers to pledge that they fully understand the perils associated with impaired driving. By signing the document the young driver agrees to avoid alcohol and drugs, to never ride with an impaired driver, and to always wear their seat belt. The final part of the agreement for the teen driver is to promise to call their parents if they are ever in a situation that compromises their own personal safety. The parent must pledge the same commitment as well as to provide sober transportation home if the teen is ever in a situation that threatens their safety. Both parent and teenager must sign the document. This commitment has opened up vital and necessary conversation between adults and teenagers. This is a discussion all parents and guardians must engage in with their children on a continuing basis. No matter what your thoughts are concerning alcohol abuse, if you are under the age of 21 it is illegal to consume alcohol in most states. Always remember; drinking and driving related collisions are the number one killer of young drivers. This message must be instilled in our young drivers along with open and honest conversations about the dangerous effects of drinking and driving.

Many states are now adopting laws that can suspend a new driver's licenses if found with any amount of alcohol in their blood stream. Some licenses can be suspended until the driver turns

21. DWI/DUI (Driving While Intoxicated and Driving Under the Influence) in most states is .08 on the blood alcohol scale. That is roughly four drinks in a one hour period. Many states also have laws prohibiting as little as two drinks in an hour which is referred to as Driving While Ability Impaired. These laws carry hefty fines as well as suspension and revocation of your driving privileges. For repeat offenders it can mean jail time and permanent loss of driving privileges. Make sure you know the laws of your state. Not driving at all after drinking seems to be the best and easiest solution to the problem. Designating a non-drinking driver to provide safe transportation is one way to avoid a DWI or perhaps even a serious collision. Other options include calling someone to come pick you up, using a taxi service, or perhaps even spending the night. In any event a clear cut plan must be established before heading out on a night of drinking. A commitment to safety must be made by everyone involved.

In summary every parent and guardian must have this important discussion with their child. Understanding your own states laws as well understanding the serious consequences of intoxicated driving must be discussed openly and honestly. The use of the SADD contract is great way to begin this discussion and to help reinforce the commitment to alcohol and drug free driving. Remember this contract is for both the adult and the young driver. Adults need to make the same commitment and serve as a good role model at all times. Develop your plan, sign a contract, and stick to it. This will go a long way in the prevention of alcohol related collisions.

CHAPTER 6: DISTRACTED DRIVING

Just as we begin to make some progress in the battle with alcohol and driving, a new enemy has come to the forefront. That enemy is the rapid rise of mobile technology and social media. This new enemy of our roadways has hit the ground running, and is quickly approaching alcohol related fatalities as our nation's largest problem. Just glancing down to check your phone for a split second is all that it takes to cause a fatal car crash. The fact is that around twenty eight percent of all driving fatalities of young adults ages 16-25 involve texting and driving. At no time should any driver be distracted from their primary mission of keeping their vehicle safe on the roads.

States have once again reacted to this new concern by adopting cell phone laws. These laws are a work in progress since modern phones are now used for texting, making phone calls, as well as being used as GPS units and reading devices. The emergence of hands free systems has also come into existence to help solve this growing problem. Unfortunately many new studies have shown that by simply talking while driving can be as equally distracting as holding a phone to your ear. Anything that distracts you from the driving task creates a serious consequence for you and all the drivers around you. Your problem becomes their problem. Let's look at the many forms of distracted driving:

1. Talking on the cell phone
2. Eating or drinking
3. Looking at passengers
4. Adjusting temperature
5. Turning lights on and off
6. Adjusting radio or mp3 device
7. Smoking
8. Looking at map or directions
9. Sending or receiving electronic messages
10. Taking notes
11. Applying make up
12. Shaving (believe it or not)
13. Combing or brushing hair
14. Looking for street signs in a strange area

ZERO TOLERANCE

There is only one solution to this ever growing distraction problem, and that is zero tolerance. The simple and clear direction to give to every new driver is simply to avoid all distractions while driving. The temptation is great, but the habit of avoidance instantly makes you a better driver.

Mobile devices seem to be the biggest distraction to young drivers based on the high incidence of tech related collisions. Again your best plan is to lock up that mobile device, or leave it at home in order to prevent the temptation. If you must use a cell phone or some other device, pull over to a safe place well off the road. A plan similar to that of a designated driver would be to use another passenger in the car to aid as your "designated texter." Do whatever it takes, but keep the device out of the driver's hands. When navigating a 2000 pound vehicle, a short distraction can become fatal distraction.

As far as eating, drinking and grooming in the car, simply get up earlier and do these things at home before ever getting into a vehicle. Any vehicle control that needs to be adjusted should be done quickly so not to distract you from your primary mission of watching the road. GPS devices are great trip planning tools. The safest strategy for planning a road trip is having your plan mastered and reviewed before you venture out on your journey. Having a responsible "co-pilot" is the best option. Taking a "lifeguard" mentality when talking to your passengers is the best way to stay focused on your driving. This simply means keeping your eyes focused on the task of driving at the same time you are talking to someone in the car. When you are trying to locate streets and businesses in an unknown area it is best to get directions, and study them before you even leave the house. Having landmarks and street names will keep you from making last minute lane adjustments.

The final ingredient needed in order to help resolve the distracted driving problem is the adult driver themselves. When experienced adult drivers get behind the wheel they are acting as a role model for our younger generation. Every habit and action is scrutinized by the teen driver. Whether you like it or not, you are an ever present model for all new drivers. So, if you have bad driving habits, work hard to change them. At the same time you are role modeling, you will also become a better driver. Changing a bad habit is not easy. It is something that must be practiced over and over again. Learning the right way at the start is much more practical. So let's make it easier on all new drivers by teaching them the right lessons now. This way, bad habits will never be established.

Chapter 7: Emergency Procedures

By learning and executing the skills of *following distance*, *visual lead time* and isolated driving, you have already taken some of the most significant steps to avoid a collision. By using these skills in your everyday driving, you have greatly reduced your chances of being involved in an accident. Knowledge about emergency situations are equally as important. There are two basic types of emergencies that any new driver may encounter. The first emergency, and probably the most common, is driver error. The second is car or vehicle failure. A beginning driver must be prepared mentally and physically to deal with these two crucial situations. In any emergency situation it is important to stay calm and not to panic. Being prepared and executing proper driving technique will enhance your ability to handle any emergency situation.

Driver Error

A well-seasoned defensive driver may even occasionally make a mistake. Unpredictable actions by other drivers can also create an emergency situation. Understanding and identifying the emergency early is the key to avoiding the collision. Remember you always have three controls over your car that can help you in most any situation. Those three controls are braking, steering, and acceleration. You may need to use one or more of these controls in order to handle the majority of emergencies that you may encounter. During these emergencies you always want to plan for the least evasive escape route. This is the route that will cause the least amount of damage to the driver, passengers, pedestrians, and animals as well as other vehicles and their passengers'. The best approach to determine the easiest escape route is to identify a problem early within your visual lead time, and by using your brakes to control the situation. The second more dangerous condition is when you have no choice but to lock up the brakes. This may be seen in such circumstances as avoiding a deer, or a car that pulls out in front of you at the very last second. Whatever the situation, panic must be avoided, and your escape route must be properly executed.

In some cases, steering right or left is the obvious choice in collision avoidance. Since we live in the US, and we drive on the right hand side of the road, steering right is the logical choice in most cases. Steering left, more often than not will create a head on collision. Examples such as a vehicle approaching in your lane, or a driver running a red light from the left side of the intersection, make steering right the best decision. When a vehicle runs a stop sign or a red light from the right side, steering left may become your only escape choice. Sometimes the safest decision may involve the use of braking and steering in combination.

Probably the least used car control in an emergency situation is the gas pedal. However; when the gas pedal is needed you must be prepared to use it. A loss of brakes situation of the car or truck behind you is the most obvious time to use acceleration as the proper escape route. If the road is clear ahead, and the intersections aren't blocked, then accelerate and get off the road as quickly as you can. If a rear end collision cannot be avoided, then make sure to release your brakes to help soften the impact. Braking after the collision will keep you from hitting any other objects in your path.

Vehicle Failure

Vehicle equipment failures can happen at any time and without warning. Brakes can fail, engines can overheat or perhaps even stall, and steering systems can stop working. The best recipe to prevent vehicle failure is to have your car properly maintained at the manufacturer's suggested intervals. Yearly inspections go a long way in identifying vehicle problems. However; it is always a good idea to prepare for the worst. Let's take a look at some of the more common equipment failures and how to deal with them.

Loss of Brakes

Nothing is scarier than depressing the brakes and nothing happens. If this occurs there are some very logical steps to take in order to avoid a collision.

1. Pump the brakes to build up pressure in the brake lines. Most vehicle brakes are hydraulic which means they require brake fluid.
2. If that doesn't work try shifting to a lower gear. This creates "engine drag" and will slow your vehicle down more gradually.
3. If those two actions fail to solve the problem, then it is time to use the emergency brake. If your emergency brake is located between the seats and has a handle and a release button, then you need to use the apply-release method. What this means is that you want to depress the release button on the brake handle, and alternately apply pressure and then release. Applying the handle too abruptly may lock the wheels and cause a spin out. If your emergency

brake is located on the driver side floor then you will need to try a different approach. Pull out on the release handle as you slowly and smoothly depress the emergency brake. Gradually give in with release handle as you depress the emergency brake to create a smooth stop. Once again do not just depress the emergency brake pedal only, since it will cause total wheel lock up.

TIRE BLOWOUT

Losing tire air pressure and tire blowout are very similar, but are dealt with in very different ways. If your tire loses air pressure keep a firm grip on the wheel, check traffic behind you and get safely off the road. Call someone or perhaps even an auto service for help. If you know how to change a tire make sure you are completely off the road, and warn other drivers behind you with either cones or flares. Make sure your car is completely off the road on a flat surface. In the event of a tire blowout, air pressure is lost quickly and may even create an explosion. Here are the logical emergency steps for the handling of a tire blow out:

1. Hold tightly to the steering wheel.
2. Steer straight ahead
3. Ease up on the accelerator pedal

4. Do not brake until the car is under control. Braking early could cause the car to swerve and go out of control.

HANDLING A SKID

A skid can happen at any time and in a variety of situations. Ice, snow, wet pavement and loose gravel are all situations that offer the potential to skid. The best defense is to make sure you have the appropriate tires for the region of the country that you live in. Be sure to maintain proper tire tread depth. Proper tire tread depth is 2/32 of an inch. To measure your tread depth simply put a Lincoln head penny into the tread of the tires; if you can see the top of Lincoln's head you need new tires. Good tire tread will help reduce the severity of a skid as well as decreasing the chance of hydroplaning. Here are the steps in handling a skid:

1. Reduce your speed but do not apply the brakes.
2. Turn your wheels into the direction of the skid and continue to do this until the car straightens out. This is called counter steering. Another way to say it is to try to keep your front wheels ahead of you rear wheels. Keep the front wheels heading in the direction you want to go.

3. Continue to repeat this procedure until you have gained total control of your car.

OTHER DRIVING EMERGENCIES

There are many other emergencies that every new driver should be prepared for even though these situations may not be quite as common. Steering failure is one of those. New cars are made so well these days, that problems that we faced thirty years ago are no longer a factor. In case you do lose your steering make sure you ease up on the gas pedal. Do not shift or brake in this situation. Shifting and braking will cause the car to be out of balance and perhaps send you into a spin. As the car begins to slow you may use the brake.

A stuck accelerator pedal is another one of those situations that does not happen too often. But if it does, try to pry the pedal up with your toe. If that doesn't work shift the car to neutral and brake it down gradually. Again, in this situation braking and shifting to a lower gear may cause an uncontrollable skid.

Running off the pavement can also be a tense situation. If this happens stay on the shoulder and ease up on the gas. After you have slowed down, steer gently back onto the pavement. If the shoulder is a steeper grade you may have to steer more sharply at an angle to return to your lane.

I have only scratched the surface of the many problems and emergencies that new and adult drivers alike may encounter during their driving careers. Remember… your best defense is never to panic and to utilize the defensive driving skills laid out for you in this book.

Chapter 8: Attitude and Aggressive Driving

I have saved the shortest and perhaps the most important chapter for last. You can be the most skilled driver in the world. You can be the best defensive driver in the world. However; if you don't have the proper attitude each and every time you get behind the wheel, these skills mean nothing. Attitude controls our behavior and influences the way we react to every situation. All other distractions in our life have to be let go when we get behind the wheel. Failing a test, or breaking up with a girlfriend, are two examples of situations that could have a negative effect on driving. Driving is a skill that requires 100% of our focus and attention… 100% of the time. Our mind must be clear and free of any distractions that could influence our decision making in a negative way. When you are behind the wheel you need to be relaxed so you can concentrate on the task at hand.

Avoid stressful situations at all costs. Listening to relaxing music and deep breathing exercises can be used to relieve stress. Planning ahead and allowing yourself plenty of time to reach your destination will help you to stay calm. If you are running late do not speed to make up this time.

Going five miles an hour faster in a one hour period is roughly five minutes. Is being five minutes late really worth speeding? Controlling the mind, and staying within a positive attitude, will make you a better driver.

AGGRESSIVE DRIVING

Most police departments define aggressive driving as, "operating a motor vehicle in a selfish, bold or pushy manner without regard for the rights or safety of other drivers and pedestrians." Aggressive driving can very quickly escalate into road rage. Examples of aggressive driving include tailgating, frequent lane changes, speeding and violating traffic laws. Aggressive driving becomes road rage when a driver yells, curses, gestures or perhaps honks their horn at another driver. These verbal provocations can quickly escalate into road rage. Pursuing or ramming another vehicle are just a couple examples of extreme road rage. Obviously the drivers in these types of situations have not learned how to control their emotions and attitudes.

Teenage drivers as well as adult drivers can avoid being victims of aggressive driving and road rage by doing a few simple things.

1. Avoid eye contact with the aggressive driver.
2. Ignore and avoid rude gestures.
3. Get out of their way. Let them pass and do not retaliate.
4. Continue to be a courteous defensive driver

You may not be able to change someone else's aggressive mindset, but you can definitely control yours. Put your ego aside when faced with an aggressive driver, and concentrate on the task at hand. A good positive attitude when behind the wheel is necessary in order to become a safe and defensive driver.

Chapter 9: A Lifesaving Checklist

I have designed Chapter Nine to provide you with a quick reference of the skills that need to be taught to your teenage driver each and every day. You may access a downloadable checklist from my website at **www.driveredcoach.com** Make a copy and place it in your glove box to serve as a constant reinforcement to your young driver. Remember to refer back to the necessary chapter to obtain a more detailed explanation of each skill or strategy.

1. The Basics

Remember to get your hands high on the wheel: 9 o'clock, 3 o'clock or above, but not together! Use the right foot for braking. Don't forget to signal, use your mirror, and check your blind spot on all lateral maneuvers. Always in that order!

2. Following Distance

Remember you want a two second following distance for speeds of forty five miles an hour or less. Increase that time to four seconds for speeds over forty five. In bad weather you may need six or eight seconds of following distance.

3. Visual Lead Time

How far you look down the road helps you to keep your car in a straight line path as well as forecast any problems you may encounter down the road. Twelve seconds is the accepted lead time for speeds of forty five mile or less. Twenty seconds is best for speeds of forty five miles an hour or more. At night remember not to "overdrive" your headlights. In other words, drive faster than your headlights project.

4. Safety Restraints

Always buckle your seat belt to help prevent the second collision. Also remember to lock your doors and adjust your headrest to the middle of your head.

5. Alcohol

Have the discussion and sign the SADD Contract agreeing that you will never get behind the wheel after the consumption of alcohol. Both parent and teenager must sign the agreement.

Always have a plan and stick to it in order to avoid getting behind the wheel after drinking.

6. Cell Phone

Zero tolerance, leave the cell phone home or lock it up. If you absolutely must use it pull over to a safe location out of traffic.

7. Vehicle Emergencies

Go over the vehicle emergencies in chapter seven and memorize each one. Remember not to panic. A good following distance and visual lead time will go a long way in preventing collisions.

8. Attitude

Get your attitude under control before getting in your vehicle, and then maintain this positive attitude as you drive. Allow nothing to bother you. You control the way you react to any and every situation.

Driver Education Resources

You can get plenty of free information regarding all topics in the field of driver education by going to **www.driveredcoach.com**. On this website you will find information where you can learn the latest techniques of driving as well the important skills needed to help you pass your road test.

I hope you found "Save Your Teenage Driver's Life" helpful and will continue to use the book in reinforcing the important skills needed to become a safe and defensive driver. My intention in writing this book was based on a hope to prevent, or perhaps even save, a young driver's life from the perils of a fatal traffic collision. Parents must create a partnership with both the driver education professionals as well as their teenage driver. After the skills are taught, and your teenager feels a mastery level of knowledge you must continue to reinforce all that you have learned throughout your driving careers.

As a way of expressing my thanks for your purchase, I am offering a free guide to help your teen pass their road test. Just go to **www.driveredcoach.com** to claim your free guide. Add your email to get special offers and updates on future publications and courses.

THANK YOU!

I hope you enjoyed "Save Your Teenage Driver's Life" as much as I enjoyed writing the book for you. I know you could have purchased many other books on the topic of traffic safety, but you selected mine and these strategies will forever be part of your on road driving skills. If you believed my book helped you I would really appreciate you leaving a short honest review of this book on the Amazon website.

This feedback will allow me to continue writing Kindle books that produce positive results. So if you enjoyed "Save Your Teenage Driver's Life" let me know. Thanks again for purchasing and reading my book. Keep an eye out for future titles in the Driver and Traffic Safety field as well as several titles in the Health, Fitness and Wellness fields.

Check these other books out by Hank Wysocki on Amazon:

"Teach Your Teenager How to Drive a Car": *Sequential Lessons for a New Driver*

"New York State Driver's License Practice Test Questions and Study Guide": *Learn How to Drive Safely and Pass the Permit Test*

Made in the USA
Lexington, KY
05 February 2019